To order additional copies, please contact:
The CreateSpace Shop at
www.createspace.com
or
www.amazon.com

£2

OUR LADY of QUITO

Queen of Ecuador

Dolorosa Press

Our Lady of Quito
Queen of Ecuador

We are going to relate a prodigious event that occurred on April 20th, 1906 in the capital of Ecuador, and which the ecclesiastical authorities, after meticulous examination, declared to be a miracle. But before, for a better understanding of this, we recall the historical circumstances.

Ecuador was the first nation that officially consecrated itself to the Sacred Heart of Jesus on March 25, 1874 and on August 6, 1892 to the Immaculate Heart of Mary.

In the solemn consecration of 1874, read by the very important representative of the Church, Archbishop Checa y Barba, and afterwards by the president of the nation, García Moreno, was sealed an irrevocable pact: "Prostrate before your divine presence, all the public powers of the Church and of the State offer and consecrate to Thee now and for always the republic of Ecuador as Thy exclusive possession and property."[1] The pact was sealed with the blood of the president, assassinated on August 6, 1875, the First Friday, in the same church of the consecration and the same day on which he had noted in his spiritual diary: "Lord Jesus, show me what it is that I ought to do today for Thy love." Also in the same church, on Good Friday of 1877 the Archbishop was poisoned to death.

At the death of Garcia Moreno a moderate liberal, Antonio Borrero, was elected, but General Veintimilla, an extreme liberal, who was defeated in 1883, rebelled. There was a moderately lawful era until 1895. Then, an extreme liberal, General Eloy Alfaro rebelled, and remained in power for twenty years taking part in revolutions. He was a dictator from 1895 to 1901 and from 1906 to 1911 thanks to another revolution. Finally he returned to rebel against his successor in 1911, but was defeated and lynched in 1912. General Leónidas Plaza, a companion of the former, governed from 1901 to 1905, and returned to power in 1912-1916 by another rebellion… and so the countless rebellions continued.

In 1895 General Alfaro "a model of infamy" promised Pope Leo XIII to maintain harmony with the Vatican, but in the following year he broke the Concordat. He expelled the Jesuits from the Amazon region, where they had founded 152 villages. He forbade the establishment of new religious congregations in the country.

In 1900 the Ecuadorian Congress decreed the secularization of convents. It restricted the freedom of teaching, and the colleges were unable to give examinations. In the state schools it suppressed the teaching of religion. It revoked the decree of the National Consecration to the Sacred Heart.

In 1901 the government seized part of Saint Gabriel's College from the Jesuits. The following year General Plaza established civil marriage and divorce. In 1904 he forbade novitiates, and deprived the religious institutions of their goods, the slogan being: "Independence from Spain, independence from Rome."[2] In 1906, Alfaro reached the point of a complete rupture with the Church. He forbade Bishop Riera, the consecrated bishop of Portoviejo, to enter into his diocese. The constant persecution forced the number of students in Saint Gabriel's College to be reduced from 400 to 150. Not content with this, a decree was already prepared, to expel the Jesuits from the college they were operating since 1862, and it was one of the few Catholic colleges that remained. (It is the usual hellish technique: the best way to de-Christianize a country is to prevent its youth from receiving a Catholic education and formation).

Intervention of the Virgin

The Virgin chose the same college dedicated to one of the Archangels: Saint Gabriel.

The place was the dining hall of the boarding students, 72 feet (lessened by a partition to 43 feet) by 23 feet, on the first floor of the college.

The picture, a color oleograph[3] (20 inches long by 16 inches wide) of the Sorrowful Heart of Mary (Our Lady of Sorrows with her heart pieced with seven swords), printed in France. The Jesuits had purchased three of these from a traveling salesman, and one of them was placed in the dining hall, on the right side as one enters, six feet from the floor. Between it and the floor was a bench 16 inches high. The picture was one of the many pictures in the college.

The time: 8 o'clock at night on April 20th, 1906, Easter Friday.

The persons: 35 boarding students, aged between 11 and 17 years old, coming from every region of Ecuador: the Father Prefect (or head of discipline), Andrew Roesch, a Frenchman; the Brother Assistant Supervisor, Louis Alberdi, a Spaniard; and three employees. (The rector of the College was Father Andrew Machado of Cuenca, Ecuador, who would later become the bishop of Guayaquil).

Because it was the Easter vacation, the students had returned that day tired from an excursion. After a short period of study, they were brought to the two large tables of the dining hall that ran parallel to the side walls, for supper. Near the end of the meal the Father Prefect arrived and gave the "Deo gratias" (permission to speak, in place of listening to a reading), and told them the news of the terrible earthquake that had occurred on the 18th of the month in San Francisco, California. The students of the College were very familiar with this type of tragedy, as earthquakes are not uncommon in Ecuador.

The children were chatting with one another. In front of the picture of Our Lady of Quito there were three eleven year old boys, who on Holy Thursday of the previous week had made their First Communion: James Chávez, Charles Herrman, and Peter Donoso. Struck by the news of the devastation in California, Chavéz was saying that he would like to die in an earthquake, after receiving Holy Communion. Father Prefect called Donoso to his table. Herrman remained with Chavéz, who was looking at the Virgin, when… But let us ask him himself what happened next.

"We finished taking coffee, the Brother Alberdi came and told us about the earthquake in California and we began to speak about the Virgin. I said that the seven swords were driven in by our sins; and I looked at her, and she was moving her eyelids; and I thought that it was my imagination. The other boy looked afterwards and said to me, 'Look at the Virgin,' and we kept looking.

"Seeing what was happening we knelt down; we prayed an Our Father and a Hail Mary. We were looking at what was happening; I called Peter Donoso saying: 'Come and you will see this funny thing.' I called him three times. She [the Virgin] was moving her eyes, the left one and afterwards the right one; the first time she was moving them a little more quickly. After a repetition of two or three times she was closing both." This was the response of eleven-year-old Charles Herrman, in the canonical process. Let us also read that of his companion, Chávez:

"When we finished eating we said, *Deo gratias*, and we were speaking about the Virgin and the Father Prefect called one of the boys to the other table, and two of us remained alone. And then I looked upwards, and I saw that the eyes of the Virgin were beginning to tremble like someone who is in agony, and seeing this I said to the other boy, 'Let us pray an Our Father and a Hail Mary,' and we knelt down. Then we sat down again. And looking at what was happening, we informed the others and some of them came. Then we went to get the Father Prefect, but he did not want to come. Afterwards we went to get him again and he came, but he did not want to believe at all. And Brother Alberdi stood in the middle and said, "It is certain," but he [the Father Prefect] still did not want to believe, until all the boys were repeating at the same time: 'Now she opens, now she closes!' After a quarter of an hour the bell rang for us to go to the chapel before the incident ceased."

And so it began. In fact, Donoso who was in the group of the Father Prefect, when his friend Hermann came running to get him, paid no attention to him. The other boy had to invite him three times before he would get up and go: "I went over," Donoso relates, "and I saw the eyes of the Virgin moving; and I covered my eyes so as not to see, out of fear, and I went another time where Father Roesch…"

Naturally, the priest did not at all believe that the Virgin was moving her eyes; nor did he change his mind. How was he going to believe this sort of thing from boys? Brother Alberdi declared in the process, "One of the boys of the first tables came to tell us that the Virgin was moving her eyes; and we went closer coldly and with little enthusiasm, as least speaking for myself."

Likewise the other boys were stubborn in not believing or going closer, and they delayed for about a quarter of an hour. Many did this, as they later declared: "Although we did not believe, and we continued our conversation, since everyone was getting up we went to see out of curiosity." Another testified: "Upon receiving the news it made no impression upon me, and I even laughed, but curiosity got the best of me and I got closer to the Virgin." And another relates: "When we heard it said that the Virgin was opening and closing her eyes, we went with the intention of making a joke out of what they were saying. Almost all of us did not care about it. I went, but to make fun, and while shoving the others who were coming with me."

The Prefect, Father Roesch, declared in his turn: "With great insistence another boy came to urge me to go to see what was happening. At first I refused what they asked saying that he should stop the nonsense, because it seemed to me to be an illusion of the boys; but finally, because of the urging and the calling by all those who were witnessing the prodigy, I went over to the table that was located closest to the picture, with the resolution formed of dispelling the notion. I verified with much determination that the electric lights were not moving, or if some beam was reflecting on the image; none of this appeared.

"Standing in front of the image surrounded by the children, I fixed my eyes on her, without blinking, and I observed that the Most Holy Virgin was slowly closing her eyes; but still not believing that I was certain, I left the place. The Brother, who was more certain than I, seeing this, said to me, amazed at what was happening, "But Father, what if this is a miracle? What if this is a miracle..." I returned again to the spot where I previously was; then I felt a coldness that chilled my body, while seeing, without any possible doubt, that the picture was actually closing and opening its eyes. When this was happening all the children that were watching the prodigy were crying out with one voice, 'Now she closes; now she opens; now the left.' But it should be noted that at times she was closing only the left eye or at least more clearly than the right, since it appeared to be more closed. The prodigy repeated itself several times and lasted a little more or less than fifteen minutes. It ceased when, seeing that it was already very late for the night prayers, and always fearing to give too much attention, I gave the signal for the students to retire; which they did very much to their regret, since they wanted to kneel and pray. I forbade any noise that would cause a disturbance, since it seemed to me that if the prodigy was miraculous the witnesses would not be lacking to prove it. At first I believed it to be an illusion, and afterwards I was seen going away still without giving credit. Urged again by the Brother, I returned, and the blinking was so evident to me, that it gave me the feeling of a chill, and I remain in this conviction."

As can be seen, they all were incredulous at the beginning. The first one who said that he saw the miracle, Charles Hermann, did not believe his eyes, for which reason neither did he make any comment to his companion, James Chávez. The latter was the first that told someone else about it.

Father Roesch not only was incredulous, he feared being influenced by the extraordinary and, incomprehensibly—it proves his objectivity—, he gave the signal to go to the chapel to pray the rosary when the Virgin was continuing to open and close her eyes. And when Brother Herman Alberdi suggested to him: "Let us take the picture of the Virgin to the chapel so that we can pray the rosary in front of her," he did not consent. Likewise he neither permitted a boy, determined to inform the Father Rector, to do it. Even more, he told the students not to say anything to anyone.

Nevertheless, as soon as they left the dining hall, immediately the news spread throughout the house. Some priests did not refrain from coming to the dining hall, but nothing extraordinary happened. The picture of the Sorrowful Virgin, with her heart transpierced, had the same eyes as always. The phenomenon had ceased, or had it really?

Verification of the Testimonies

What would you have done, dear reader, if you had to pass judgment upon what was being said? Of course, before proving all this, you would need to investigate. How? By interrogating the witnesses— you will say—, by examining their credibility, the possibility of fraud, a collective suggestion, an optical illusion…

Well, the ecclesiastical authority did this, and with all the rigor of the "devil's advocate." Seven days after the event the canonical process began, without the participation of any Jesuits, it appointed a commission of scientists and another of doctors. They would take a thorough declaration from each one of the forty witnesses, and under oath. (Considering whom they were dealing with and about what they were dealing with, were the forty witnesses going to be in agreement about swearing falsely?)

At that moment, the current Vicar Capitular[4]— the diocese was vacant— ordered on April 27th that "the aforesaid picture be concealed and nothing be publicized in the press or from the pulpit relating to this event, as long as its validity and authenticity have not been decided."

An ever prudent temporary prohibition, yet for the miracle to be verified, this heartless prohibition had been maintained indefinitely. As a matter of fact, at the same time, he named the theologians and the scientists who would conduct the investigation. They were strict (meriting later the praises of the Sacred Congregation), but not too slow: they took one month.

On the 29th, in the study hall of the boarding students the instruction of the process began. The Vicar Capitular, accompanied by the Secretary of the Chancellery and of the Senior Notary, reunited the forty witnesses and commanded that each one, without communicating with the rest of the others, write what it was that he saw, in such a way that he would be able to confirm it under oath. On the first of May a canon was commissioned as instructor Judge, assisted by the Senior Notary, and on the 5th of May they appeared in person, for: 1) the examination of the written statements, 2) their ratification under oath, 3) to propose to the witnesses a series of questions: if during those days they had heard something about that matter, if there was sufficient light, if at the beginning they were afraid and later at peace, and what effect had been produced in him and his conduct.

Concerning these statements, all agreed on the reality of the phenomenon, and it seems that at the beginning they were trying not to admit it. Someone went up to the picture, another went up to the partition to see it more closely. There was enough light (the room was illuminated by four light bulbs producing 16 foot-candles each) and the exclamations in unison: "now she opens, now she closes," lasting for more that a quarter of an hour, leave no room for doubts. "The existence of a marvelous prodigy is evident," concluded the instructor judge of the process. All also confirmed that the movement of the eyes was always full of majesty, and when opening them her gaze remained steadfast.

Once the event had been proved, the commission of scientists, after having sworn to work truthfully and diligently, reconstructed the scene in the same place, at the same hour, with the same circumstances, and examined the picture… about which fact "the subscribers will deduce: that the aforesaid phenomenon could not have occurred as the result of the light nor other physical conditions in which the picture was located. Moreover the movement of the eyes occurred many times in each instance, as proven by the fact that everyone present observed it at the same time; and its size is such that at the distance of the onlookers a movement of the eyelids could be perceived with no room for doubt; nor could it be an optical illusion because it was seen simultaneously by all…"

Was there something that remained to be proven? Yes, the mental health of the forty eyewitnesses, which is what the medical commission carried out. From the 17th to the 19th of May two eminent doctors examined each one separately and by himself. The examinations were lengthy, the result of which was, in brief: that they all possessed good health without any nervous illness or predisposition towards such phenomena, but it was just the opposite, as far as excluding any influence, no one tried to influence anyone, nor was it admissible that the youngest boys in particular were able to trick all the rest. The only one who would have had the power to do this, by his authority, was the one most hesitant to believe and he even took the students away from there.

After all these preceding events the committee of nine theologians studied in their turn the case and reported favorably. Finally the Vicar Capitular, mindful of all the above, pronounced the final word:

Pastoral Resolution

"1. The incident that took place on April 20 at the College of the Jesuit Fathers is proven to be historically certain. 2. The prodigy, under the circumstances in which it took place, *can not be explained by natural laws*. 3. This prodigy, as much on account of what preceded it as by what followed it, *can not be attributed to any diabolical influence*. In consequence *one can believe it, with a purely human faith; and one may offer the picture which occasioned it the public veneration permitted by the Church, and to pray before it with legitimate confidence*. Given at the Archiepiscopal Palace on May 31, 1906." The ecclesiastical authority officially authenticated the picture on June 10.

On the same May 31, the Vicar Capitular gave an exhortation to the faithful:

"The occurrence of which we treat," he was saying, "has presented itself with so many and such serious motives of rational credibility that although one can cease to believe it without sin, it seems difficult for anyone to reject it without straying from the norms of the most rigorous criteriology."

And he commented, "It is not possible to pass over in silence certain circumstances. The youths are witnesses to that fact that they begin to live in a world trying to deny the supernatural and at the very time when attempts are increasing to uproot from the hearts of the youth every vestige of the faith.

"On the other hand the marvelous phenomenon is caused by a simple and pious image of the Sorrowful Virgin, a favorite advocation of Ecuadorians, and especially during times of calamities it appeals to the devotion and the heartfelt sympathy of all the faithful. God has sought to make known what is not useless, but that supplication has been heard quite literally with which we so many times invoke the Heart of Mary saying to her, 'Turn thy eyes of mercy towards us.' She has indeed turned them, so tearful and tender; she has shown herself a Mother, because mothers have the secret of communicating with a look, of speaking with their eyes to their children, of teaching them, of encouraging them, of admonishing them, with just a look. Will it be a look of affection or of sad forebodings which Mary has directed to our youth?"

The Effects of the Miracle

The look of our Mother was not of sad forebodings. In the first place, for the seers it was a great spiritual impulse. They themselves declared that they had noticed it in their conduct and piety. Some were not falling asleep when reciting the rosary, others had made the resolution of avoiding sins, and to communicate more frequently. Father Prefect also noticed it: "The effect that was produced upon the children was for the better: They have formed a group or association that aims at combating bad conversations, and they did this spontaneously, and their fervor and good conduct has greatly improved." The very next day, April 22, they made a collection for putting a better frame on the picture.

Fervor was not only in those students, but in all their followers, being greatly devoted to the Sorrowful Mother of the College. And overflowing the College, it spread throughout all Quito, through all Ecuador, where her image is found on most of the hearths, and finally through all the world, especially in England, Ireland, Scotland, Spain, the United States, Columbia, Panama, Australia, Africa… St. Pius X approved the process and requested a copy of the image, which he placed on the desk in his office.

It is enough that the Mother of God opened and closed her eyes for the city to have felt itself shaken and the government bewildered. The decree of expulsion of the Jesuits went to the wastebasket. And did the rulers convert? There are some, like the brothers of the rich man, who do not convert even if the dead rise again from the dead, according to Christ's words. It is the mystery of obstinate hardness of heart, of persistence in sin, and the refusal of grace.

The Miracle Repeats Itself

The Most Holy Virgin wished to respond to the wave of enthusiasm that rose up towards her: 1) On Thursday June 7, the boarding students and several priests were in the church after supper praying the rosary before the sacred image, and when they finished they once again saw the prodigy. The bell was rung and the whole community gathered. The prodigy lasted for a quarter of an hour. Moreover the picture of the Virgin sometimes displayed profound sadness, and at other times even happiness. On the 11th, declarations were taken in the Archiepiscopal Chancellery from those who saw it. 2) On the 13th, two others say that they have seen it: Doctor Emmanuel María Salazar and his brother Nicholas. The former, who was converted, recounts in his sworn declaration that the face of the image was transformed with expressions of mildness, sweetness and love, and that "what is greater than the movement of the eyes is that she deeply moved my heart." 3) On Sunday the 24th, at 5:30 in the afternoon the prodigy repeated itself in the presence of Father Bernard, Brother Miranda, four students of the College and five students from the Christian Schools. 4) On the 26th two Dominican priests saw it. 5) On Tuesday, July 3, many people saw the miracle. 6) On July 5th, Father Alphonsus Laenen, well known and remembered in Manabi,[5] says that he saw the Virgin crying, but he is the only witness who speaks of crying.

The Veneration of Our Lady of Quito

Veneration of Our Lady of Quito, which is more properly called the Sorrowful Heart of Mary (and so it is entitled within the movement directed to her Heart advanced by herself in the last times),[6] began immediately. On Sunday June 3, a great procession was already made, with more than 10,000 people attending besides some 35,000 spectators.

On July 2 the first great Novena of Our Lady of Quito began, which is repeated every year on April 11 so as to finish on the eve of the festive anniversary of the miracle, and has always gone on growing in fervor. Not content with the annual novena, the practice was established, in Quito and in other cities, of celebrating special devotions in honor of Our Lady of Quito on the 20th day of each month. And also in 1932 the *Bulletin of Our Lady of Quito* was founded, a monthly publication to propagate her devotion.

Particularly noteworthy were the honors given to Our Lady of Quito in 1931, the silver anniversary of the miracle, which shook the entire nation; and the first Ecuadorian Marian Congress was held. The chronicles of the celebration fill four volumes. In 1934 for the first time the picture went on pilgrimage to Riobamba and other cities, generating unusual enthusiasm and tremendous excitement. The pilgrimages have been repeated. Another pilgrimage was made to Riobamba in 1938, then to Guayaquil, and to the north, to Pasto (Columbia). In 1947 the picture went to Cuenca where it remained a whole month.

In 1956, the golden anniversary of the miracle, there was a Canonical Coronation of Our Lady of Quito. Pope Pius XII in the Brief of the Coronation said: "Having consulted the Sacred Congregation of Rites, we grant by our apostolic authority and in virtue of this brief to our beloved son, Carl María de la Torre, Cardinal Priest of the Holy Church, Archbishop of Quito, that he impose in our name and with our authority, a Crown of gold upon the image of the Most Holy Virgin, the Sorrowful Mother of the College, AS QUEEN OF THE CATHOLIC EDUCATION IN ECUADOR." Dr. Camillus Ponce Enríquez, President of the Republic,[7] thanked God and Our Lady of Quito, in front of 40 diplomatic delegations, for his electoral victory.

1958. The relocation of the College of St. Gabriel to a new building was made. With the College the Picture of Our Lady of Quito will also be moved.

1978. On December 30 the National Shrine of the Sorrowful Mother is blessed and dedicated.

1981. This year marked the diamond anniversary of the miracle. In these seventy-five years, churches dedicated to our Queen and Mother have been built such as in Riobamba, Cotacachi and Ibarra. Colleges have been founded as in Loja and schools as in Llano Grande with her name. In other cities and parishes Congregations function in her honor as in Otavalo, to beg for the children and for the Ecuadorian youth.

"Once again the miraculous picture is traveling throughout the whole Republic, in towns, hospitals... The enormous interest and national fervor is impressive. Since the month of February, a program dedicated to the jubilee is transmitted daily by 46 radio transmitters and by television on Saturdays. Novenas, rosaries at dawn, and popular missions in preparation for the arrival of the Virgin take place, which increase the number of confessions and communions, with solemn Masses, in the stadiums, because the churches become too small.

One sign of the national response is the resolution of the Very Illustrious City of Ante. "Considering that it is the duty of the City to exteriorize the religious and Marian sentiment of the people that it represents, it is resolved:

> To render homage of admiration and honor to the Sorrowful Mother of the College on the diamond anniversary of the miracle of the tears shed for the country.

To give the keys of the city as a symbol of respect and admiration to the Queen of Heaven.

To recommend to all the Christian people, and particularly to the youth, devotion and love to the Sorrowful Mother of the College.

To be officially present as a group at the solemn act of her reception."

Favors of Our Lady of Quito

Our Mother is she who always begins to give us things, and to love us. "God hath first loved us" (I Jn. 4, 10), but when we come to Her, then she does her utmost, even with miracles. There would be no end in recounting all her gifts and favors: The vast majority we will know only in heaven. We are going to listen to some accounts.[8]

In the year 1917, in Ecuador, a young woman, Rose Ponce Ribadeneira was going with a group of people from Hacienda Capelo, in Sangolquí, to Santa Rosa, from the property of Mr. Jijón, when the horse on which she was riding slipped and fell to the ground, she remaining tangled in the stirrup. The horse was startled and bolted out of control, dragging along the body of the unfortunate young woman, amidst the screams of terror that the onlookers were making. One of them, Dr. Belisario Ponce, went quickly in pursuit inwardly convinced that he was not going to retrieve anything but the body of his niece in pieces; but what was his surprise when going around a curve, he noticed from afar a black shape rising up from the ground, he recognized that that it was his niece and he rushed towards her, who, as though she were insane, was muttering these words: "The Virgin has saved me. At the time I mounted I commended myself to the Sorrowful Mother of the College, and the whole way I was dragged I did not cease to cry out to the Sorrowful Mother. She has saved me." The horse ran a distance of about three hundred yards from the place where it bolted to where the dragging ended, due to the fact that the girth came off and the saddle fell to the ground; and apart from Rose having her face completely covered with dirt and her clothes in tatters, she showed absolutely no sign of the dragging. She had no wounds, not even on her face or her head.

In 1927 a boy Oswald Romero was run over by the main part of a wagon full of rocks. When falling he remembered the Mother of Sorrows. That day, after fainting and vomiting blood, he stayed asleep and afterwards was healed without medicine. He later became a priest in the United States.

In England, where she is known under the name of "Our Lady of Quito," her devotion grew greatly due to the innumerable favors that she worked during the World War, saving the houses that had her image, from the damage produced by the aerial bombardment. Even the Protestants themselves placed an image of the Sorrowful Mother in their houses and churches. Soldiers, marines and airmen carried with them small pictures so as to feel her maternal protection. Deeds such as the ones we transcribe below repeat themselves at each step.

An officer wrote to his wife, "I have just narrowly escaped death by a real miracle in North Africa. I was crossing our lines in my car in full battle. I had to travel some two miles on the open highway. A car in these circumstances is an easy target for the enemy air force. Indeed, soon after, out of some low clouds four aircraft emerged that immediately began to pursue me. They came flying at a low height behind me. At once I felt engulfed by a rain of artillery fire and machinegun fire. Suddenly, as the first result of the attack, a howitzer shell pierced the back part of the car, and after tearing my shirtsleeve and grazing my arm just below the shoulder, smashed the windshield and went on to kill a poor man who was trying to take refuge in a hole, about a hundred yards ahead. Another bullet pierced my cap, and a third snatched away from me my binoculars from my back. An artillery shot demolished one of the doors of the car, and finally it went into the ditch, pierced by six shots of artillery and riddled by gunshots; it stayed there like a sieve, but the driver and I were unhurt. Truly God has been good to me. Tell my mother that I was carrying the picture of Our Lady the Sorrow Mother of Quito in my pocket.

She is also known in Australia, where many hundreds of small pictures of the Sorrowful Mother of Quito have been distributed. There they have felt, just as in Ecuador, the compassionate hand of this Blessed Mother in the multitude of favors, such as the following, which occurred in Melbourne in 1948. A little girl fell from a balcony onto a cement floor. Having been taken to the hospital, her condition became serious. The father and mother of the girl prayed before the image of the Sorrowful Mother of Quito. She heard their prayers and in a short time the girl was completely cured.

And Mr. Ripalda likewise tells of a favor of the Virgin: "A contract with the Government of several million sucres[9] obliged me to rent an airplane from Ateca, in order to bring to Quito the commodity that had arrived from Guayaquil. Although it seemed imprudent to me to undertake the flight after six o'clock in the afternoon, because of the insistence of my friends I had to yield. When I crossed the mountains I saw that there was a torrential rain, which disturbed me; but my uneasiness was greater when I was informed in the cabin that the motors were failing and we were in serious danger. In order to save the plane, we thought of throwing the cargo to the ground, but the door did not open. I was thinking about the crash of the plane and about the ensuing death. Amidst the shadows of my distress, I placidly remembered the Sorrowful Mother of the College, to whom with the faith of a child I began to pray the Hail Holy Queen. Shortly after, a there was a tremendous jolt of the plane followed by groans of sorrow and cries of despair. I did not cease to beg the help of the Virgin, in the midst of the most complete darkness. I looked for the exit door, which gave way easily. This was the first miracle that I attributed to the Sorrowful Mother. But I believe I saw a deep abyss at my feet. Again I began to cry out to the Sorrowful Mother for help and protection. An immense wave entered into the plane, without me getting submerged within it. The plane had plunged into the Guayas River and was sinking slowly. I jumped into the water fully clothed, even wearing my hat. I thought that I was in the sea. A small boat that was providentially passing by the place of the accident saved me. By my directions the other passengers, although injured, were also rescued. The pilot and the manager of Ateca lost their lives. Days later, I thanked the Sorrowful Mother for this favor. Starting today," I said, "I believe in the Catholic religion, I believe in miracles; I would like to do something for the Sorrowful Mother in the material order; I would like above all to be henceforth a practicing Catholic. I promise to confess and receive Communion."

Better known, by the public narrations of the protagonist himself, was the following: on Thursday June 5, 1941 the North American Captain Burguess and the Ecuadorian officials Second Lieutenant Dávalos and Lieutenant Louis Arias departed from Esmeraldas for Salinas. This last man, even after very many years, remembers with all the details the tragedy while the students listen with growing emotion: "I asked the captain if they had loaded the gasoline. He assured me that even the auxiliary tanks had been filled. With this certainty I began the flight. It was four o'clock in the afternoon; we went into a storm so thick that the ends of the wings could not be seen. The motor started to stall. My fear was realized: there was no gasoline!

"Beneath my feet was the sea. The plane shook indecisively; it began to descend slowly, irremediably... I heard a hiss, a screech, a bang... We slid open the laminated windows, we took off our clothes, and put on the life jackets. The water was flooding the cabins, and so we had to abandon the plane. I found myself in the depths of the sea, surrounded by sharks and with my companions hanging on me because they do not know how to swim. The captain was driven insane out of terror, and he died at about ten o'clock. We both were perhaps hoping for the same thing.

"A splendid day dawned and it enabled me to realize that the coast was within sight. We swam with all our strength. Dávalos began to despair; finally he was silent; then, a gasp… He was dead! I clung with anxiety to the corpse. No one can imagine how useful the company of a human being is, even if it be a corpse.

"I continued like this. It was getting dark. I still kept up my morale, but my strength was diminishing. The sharks were hounding ahead threatening the corpse. Very soon a strong tug pulled us down… I could do no more… I let go of the corpse. I swam desperately; I was getting weak.

"But suddenly, as if to make my agony less painful, the picture of the Sorrowful Mother came to mind, the picture of the Virgin whom I loved so much in the College. And in the midst of the confusion I besought her; I begged God that He would not let me perish if I could still serve Him. I thought of my mother, of my brothers, and I turned to that which gives strength to a man: the faith.

"I found myself finally about 400 yards from the cliff of the coast. The undercurrent was pulling me, and after six hours of efforts, I did not succeed to get to the shore. One gigantic wave that carried me on its crest was going to break upon it. I felt that my feet were touching something; it was a rock. I grabbed on to it and left the water. My body exhausted, mangled, scorched, I did not resist any more: I fell down dismayed.

"Then another day dawned. A splash of water restored me to my senses, and I despaired. I could do no more. For a moment I was overcome by desperation. I reacted. I looked around and saw a fisherman. I wanted to shout, but my voice would not come out. The fisherman being suspicious was looking at me like a monster or a lunatic: naked, staggering, and desperate. Finally he came near. Another fisherman appeared. I was saved, thanks to the Sorrowful Mother of the College.

"Now in Quito, my only concern was to publish the miracle in which the Sorrowful Mother wished to make it evident that we have in her a true Mother."

[1] Cf. the famous indulgenced prayer written by Father Nicola Zucchi S.J. (†1670): "My Queen! My Mother! I give thee all myself, and, to show my devotion to thee, I consecrate to thee my eyes, my ears, my mouth, my heart, my entire self. Wherefore, O loving Mother, as I am thine own, keep me, defend me, **as thy property and possession**. Amen."

These words would be later incorporated into the *Prayer of Total Consecration* by St. Maximilian Kolbe: "O Immaculata, Queen of Heaven and earth, refuge of sinners and our most loving Mother, God has willed to entrust the entire order of mercy to thee. I, N___, a repentant sinner, cast myself at thy feet humbly imploring thee to take me with all that I am and have, wholly to thyself **as thy possession and property**. Please make of me, of all my powers of soul and body, of my whole life, death and eternity, whatever most pleases thee. If it pleases thee, use all that I am and have without reserve, wholly to accomplish what was said of thee: 'She will crush your head,' and, 'Thou alone have destroyed all heresies in the whole world.'

"Let me be a fit instrument in thine Immaculate and merciful hands for introducing and increasing the maximum in all the many strayed and indifferent souls, and thus help extend as far as possible the blessed Kingdom of the most Sacred Heart of Jesus. For wherever thou enters, one obtains the grace of conversion and growth in holiness, since it is through thy hands that all graces come to us from the most Sacred Heart of Jesus."

[2] It is a key phrase for understanding the hidden conspiracies that direct history. The attack on the Church, Christ's kingdom, an attack directed without ceasing by the prince of this world ("the two standards," following St. Ignatius, in the perpetual battle), has reached in the last centuries the main political powers that favored the Church: the Spanish empire, the Austrian-Hungarian empire (World War I), the French and the Portuguese colonial empire (World War II)… —thus dealing a hard blow to the Catholic missions. The consequences have been terrible.

Which are the hidden hands? Today it will be above all the KGB, the Russian antichrist, which finances — without money it would be impossible— the terrorist movements and many pro-independence movements, by getting a fifth column of traitors in every country: resentful, ambitious, naïve (not without any benefit)… Since the 18th century Masonry (in its various branches) also introduced itself into Spain on this side and on the other side of the ocean, and was the great motivator of liberal antireligious "change," about which these same men are vainglorious and for any reason they denounced the Popes and Catholic historians. (There are many enlightening facts, e. g. the letters of Napoleon to the lodges of North America so that they stir up rebellion in the Spanish lands overseas, by exaggerating the defects of the unitary government, defects which will always be had, but whose remedy is worse than the sickness, inasmuch as the present day economic and religious sluggishness proves that united countries were the most advanced. Why will one not study history more?

Of course the takeover of power in our countries by antichristian governments, and the consequent national decadence, is a punishment for sins. The thesis is insupportable (e. g. of Aranguren) that countries by being Catholic are more underdeveloped than Protestant countries, as if God treats His better children worse. Nor is it admissible, for the same reason, the "martyr" theory: namely that Spain bleed itself through defending Catholicism against the Protestants; it bled itself more in the Reconquest, and its fight for the Cross had as its reward an empire.

It is necessary to loudly proclaim these truths and historical criterions, in order to wake up sleeping consciences without any ideals. To eliminate the infuriating scandal that Catholic countries have submitted to anti-Catholic laws in education, the family, and worship… by a minority: that says it is defending liberty. The situation has to change, and we hope soon, when the promise of Fatima has been accomplished: "In the end my Immaculate Heart will triumph" and "Thy kingdom come" will be accomplished, with the conversion of Russia and the reunification of the Spanish peoples under Christ ("I will reign in Spain"), as a condition for carrying out our evangelical world-wide mission, to which we are called by the unmerited grace and divine predilection, through the mediation of Holy Mary.

[3] An oleograph is a lithograph printed in oil colors to imitate an oil painting.

[4] A Vicar Capitular is the administrator of a vacant diocese.

[5] Manabi is a western province of Ecuador on the coast.

[6] See the booklet: *Fatima. El Corazón de María,* especially pp. 24 and following.

[7] He was the first conservative candidate elected to the presidency after 64 years of liberal government. He had studied in the College of St. Gabriel for his high school studies and was president of the Republic of Ecuador from 1956-1960.

[8] God wishes that His "feats" or extraordinary interventions be told (Cf. Is. 12; Ps. 9, 77, 85, 104, 117, 144 etc.) and this is an act of worship. There is no room for doubt that, like a good sermon, it makes an impression upon the faithful, it helps them to be better, and to go to God. That "superior" attitude that "disregards" miracles, by making them seem related to one's inadequate education, is part of the global strategy of the prince of this world to hunt down such nuisances: by disparaging all that which is traditional, "gratifying the ears with novelties," and desecrating and pernicious novelties at that, without Confession or Eucharistic life, nor penances, nor miracles, not consequently asking them from God.

[9] The currency of Ecuador was formerly in sucres.

Himno a la Dolorosa

Chorus:

Madre Mía Dolorosa
Que nunca podré olvidar
Virgen que como un lucero
Me alumbras desde ese Altar
Bajo tu manto sagrado
Mi madre aquí me dejo
Señora ya eres mi Madre
No me abandone tu amor

Solo:

Hoy soy tu hijo, Hoy yo te adoro
Hoy te prometo, Perenne fe
Pero mañana, Dentro de un año
Dentro de veinte, Ay! Te querré?

Chorus:

Estrella salvadora,
es Madre tu semblante
Misero navegante,
naufragare sin ti
Cuando la mar del mundo
Con zozobrante quilla
Surcare mi barquilla
Acuérdate de mi

Aunque avance rugiendo la tormenta
Y en mi mástil ya gima el huracán
Feliz con tu recuerdo soberano

Desafío las olas de la mar
Me arrollaran quizás entre su espuma
Mas negar que me amaste y que te ame
Negar que fui tu hijo y que en tus brazos
Se paso como un sueño mi niñez
Eso nunca lo haré Madre querida
Eso nunca lo haré

Hymn to Our Lady of Quito

Chorus:

My Sorrowful Mother
whom I can never forget
Virgin who like a bright star
doest shine upon me from this altar,
under thy sacred mantle
my mother left me here:
O Lady, thou art now my Mother,
may thy love never abandon me!

Solo:

Today I am your son,
Today I honor thee
today I promise you
endless fidelity;
but tomorrow,
within a year,
within twenty,
Oh!... Will I seek thee?

Chorus:

A star of salvation
is, O Mother, thy countenance;
I, a wretched navigator,
will be shipwrecked without thee…
When the sea of the world,
with its capsizing keel,
my little boat will cross
remember me!
remember me!

Even though the storm comes howling
and on my mast the hurricane now wails,
happy with your sovereign remembrance
I defy the waves of the sea…
Perhaps they will roll me amidst their froth,
but to deny that thou loved me and that I loved thee,
to deny that I was thy son and that in thy arms
I passed my childhood like a dream,
this never will I do, dear Mother,
this never will I do.

Oración a la Dolorosa

Oh Madre Dolorosa!
por tus lagrimas,
Por la corona de espinas,
por los clavos que llevas en tus manos,
por las espadas de dolor
con que nuestros pecados
traspasaron tu Corazón
vuelve a nosotros esos tus ojos misericordiosos
y alcanzanos de tu Hijo Santísimo
dolor intenso de nuestras culpas
y vivos sentimientos de fe, esperanza y caridad

Oh! Madre Dolorosa
Protege a la Santa Iglesia,
Protege a nuestra Patria,
Ampara a la juventud
Ampara a la niñez.
Amen

Prayer to the Sorrowful Mother of the College

Oh, Sorrowful Mother!
by your tears,
by the crown of thorns,
by the nails that you carry in your hands,
by the swords of sorrow
with which our sins
transpierced your Heart
turn towards us those eyes of mercy of yours
and obtain from your Most Holy Son
intense sorrow for our sins
and lively sentiments of faith, hope and charity.

Oh, Sorrowful Mother!
Protect the holy Church,
Protect our country,
Protect the youth
Protect the children.
Amen.

PHOTOS

Photo of Father Andrew Roesch and Brother Louis Alberdi and the thirty four boys of the College of St. Gabriel who first saw the miracle before the miraculous image. The three first Communicants who first saw the miracle are seated next to the the priest and brother.

Procession of the Picture of Our Lady of Quito with the College students on the 50th anniversary of the prodigy. There were 100,000 people in attendance.Pope Pius XII sent a vibrant radio message.

The refectory where the miracle took place on April 22, 1906. A partition separates the kitchen from the refectory from the kitchen. The youngest boys sat near it.

The refectory has now been made a beautiful chapel.

The canonical coronation of the Sorrowful Mother of the College took place on April 22, 1956. The president of the republic, Joseph Mary Velasco Ibarra carried the crown; the Archbishop of Quito, Cardinal Charles Mary de la Torre, crowned the image (below).

In front of the main altar of Jesuit church, the Compañia, are seated:H.G. Raúl Eduardo Vela Chiriboga, Archbishop (2nd from the left);H.E. Néstor Herrera Heredia, President of the Episcopal Conference and Bishop of the diocese of Machala (3rd from the left); Dr. Alejandro Serrano Aguilar, vice-president (4th from the left); Wilfrido Lucero, President of the Congress (5th from the left); General Paco Moncayo, mayor of Quito (6th from the left); Ramiro González Jaramillo, governor of the state of Pinchincha (7th from the left).

Procession with the image escorted by present day college students on the 100th anniversary, April 22, 2006.

The picture is solemnly placed above the main altar of the Compañia, the Jesuit church adjacent to the College of St. Gabriel, after having been brought throughout all Ecuador with a procession in each city.

One of the evening Novena Processions held every year.

Day time procession through the streets of Quito on the Sunday after the 100th anniversary.